Getting Around

On Foot

Cassie Mayer

Heinemann Library
Chicago, Illinois

Customer Service   888–454–2279

Visit our website at www.heinemannlibrary.com

Photo research by Tracy Cummins
Designed by Jo Hinton-Malivoire
Printed and bound in China by South China Printing Company
10 09 08 07 06
10 9 8 7 6 5 4 3 2 1

Library of Congress Cataloging-in-Publication Data
Mayer, Cassie.
  On foot / Cassie Mayer.
    p. cm. — (Getting around)
  Includes bibliographical references and index.
  ISBN 1-4034-8393-0 — ISBN 1-4034-8400-7 (pbk.)
  1. Walking—Juvenile literature. 2. Running—Juvenile literature. I.
Title. II. Series.
  QP310.W3M39 2006
  612′.044—dc22
                                2005036562

Acknowledgments
The author and publisher are grateful to the following for permission to reproduce copyright material:
Alamy p. 8 (Craig Lovell/Eagle Visons Photography); Corbis pp. 5 (Peter Adams/Zefa), 9 (Macduff Everton), 10 (Uli Wiesmeier/Zefa), 11 (Bob Krist), 16 (Frans Lemmens/Zefa), 18 (Alison Wright), 19 (Michael S. Yamashita), 20 (Galen Rowell); Dorling Kindersley p. 22 (Andy Crawford); Getty Images pp. 4 (Errington), 6 (Lamb), 7 (Layma), 12 (Madison), 13 (Grandadam), 14 (Allison), 15 (Raymer), 17 (Griffiths Belt), 21 (Kohen), 23 (marathon runners, Grandadam), 23 (powerwalking, Madison).

Cover image of students at the Taj Mahal in India reproduced with permission of Dennis/Getty Images.
Backcover image of a mosque in Mali reproduced with permission of Peter Adams/Zefa/Cobris.

Special thanks to Margo Browne for her help with this project.

Contents

Getting Around on Foot

Every day people move from place to place.

Some people move on foot.

How People Move

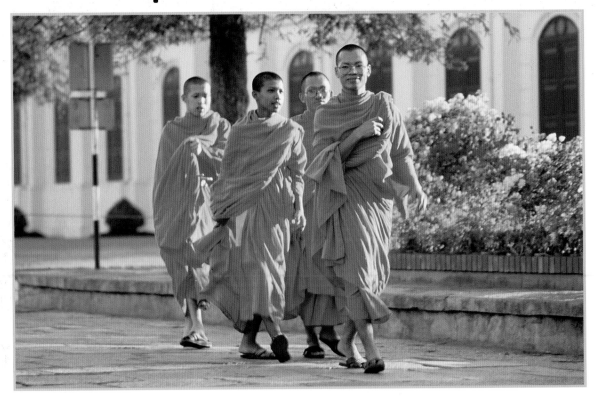

People use their feet and legs to walk.

People use their feet and legs
to run.

People walk and carry things.

People walk using animals
to carry things.

People walk long distances.

People walk short distances.

People walk to exercise.

People run in races.

Where People Go

People walk in cities.

People walk in the country.

People walk in deserts.

People walk in forests.

People walk up mountains.

People walk across rivers.

Your feet can take you
many places.